Give Value, Get Value

Everyone's a Salesperson, Let This Guide Lift You Above the Rest

Chris Whiting

Introduction

Whether you're in a business deal, a coaching session, dating, dealing with work issues, managing friendships, parenting, or making a sale, how you communicate affects your success and the lives of those around you. Across countless real-world situations in sales and life, I've learned through trial, error, and the lessons that only missteps teach.

In this guide, I distill those experiences into actionable insights designed to accelerate your learning curve, so you don't have to endure thousands of interactions to master the most important life skill: effective communication.

Chapter 1
Time, Place, and Occasion

Remember, this guide is just that, a guide. In both communication and life, perfection is a myth. Think of it like a medical practice: while every human body shares similarities, each is unique. If every doctor could treat everyone the same way, we might call it "medical perfection" rather than a "medical practice."

Context matters. Just as a doctor on the battlefield treats a broken arm differently than one in a state-of-the-art hospital, your environment, captured by Time, Place, and Occasion (TPO), should shape how you communicate. The most effective communicators are those who instinctively evaluate TPO, a skill honed through years of experience.

Before every conversation, pause and consider the TPO. This simple act can help you self-correct and avoid common missteps. Remember that no sales guide can offer a robotic, one-size-fits-all formula for success. Life is full of diverse interactions, and flexibility, along with awareness, is the key to mastering communication.

Imagine it's Friday at 8:00 PM at your holiday work party. You've likely seen, or will see, someone who fails to recognize that this setting is no different from your regular 8:00 AM Monday company meeting.

Picture a parent running batting practice for ten-year-olds, while another parent seethes on the sidelines, furious the volunteer coach didn't spot their child's "pro-level" talent. Or think about the dynamics at play during a first sales meeting, a first date, your first day on the job, or a C-Suite meeting. In each instance, your approach to TPO should be tailored to the moment. Many are not.

You already understand the importance of TPO, but like many of us, you might not naturally adjust to it. **Make it a habit to pause and consciously assess TPO before every interaction.** The best communicators do this quickly and consistently, and once you adopt this practice, you'll soon reap its benefits.

Chapter 2

Red, White & Champagne

Before we go any further, let's take a step back and talk about recognizing skills both yours and others'. It's also important to understand what type of person a company values. Since this is a guide, I like to keep things simple. I'll break it down into three categories: Champagne, White Wine, and Red Wine.

Champagne Hires: The Flashy First Impression

We all know individuals who are most like Champagne. They are the life of the party: bubbly, energetic, and impossible to ignore. When they join a company, they make an immediate impact, standing out with their charisma and enthusiasm. These are the hires that get noticed quickly, make a splash, and often rise fast, but they tend to fizzle out just as quickly. Some Champagne hires move on within months, others after a few years, but one thing remains consistent: their impatience. They crave excitement and new opportunities, and when the initial thrill wears off, they start looking elsewhere. While they're not inherently better or worse than other hires, leaders need to recognize that Champagne hires have a limited shelf life. They can add tremendous energy to an organization, but they aren't the ones who build long-term stability.

White Wine Hires: The Steady Core

White Wine hires are smooth, adaptable, and reliable. They blend well into teams, rarely make waves, and maintain a steady presence within the company. They're not necessarily the superstars, but they are dependable. These individuals form the middle third of any organization the ones you can count on but who typically won't push beyond their comfort zone.

While they may not bring dramatic innovation or disruption, White Wine hires are crucial to a company's foundation. Without them, businesses would lack stability and consistency. They are the ones who ensure that things run smoothly, day in and day out.

Red Wine Hires: The Slow-Burning Stars

Red Wine hires are the hardest to recognize at first. Unlike Champagne hires, they don't dazzle immediately, and unlike White Wine hires, they don't just maintain the status quo. Instead, they evolve, improve, and refine their craft over time.

At first, you may not be able to tell what you have in a Red Wine hire. But after a few years of dedication, hard work, and continuous learning, they begin to stand out. These are your innovators, problem solvers, and long-term leaders. They don't just critique problems; they come up with solutions. They embrace change, adapt, and consistently outperform expectations.

Red Wine hires are the game-changers, the ones who transform an organization. But they are rare. Finding and identifying them requires patience, insight, and a keen eye for potential over immediate performance.

How to Identify Red Wine Hires

Finding Red Wine hires isn't easy, but here are a couple of tools that can help:

- Gather feedback from multiple levels of your organization. Sometimes, the best insights about a candidate don't come from the hiring manager but from peers, direct reports, or even administrative staff.
- Observe how they treat people in small moments the classic "watch how they treat a waiter" test. This often reveals a person's core values and behavior when they think no one is watching.

One of my favorite interview techniques is to wait until the conversation feels complete, then ask:

"What question did I not ask you that I should have?"
Then, I sit back and say nothing.

This question catches candidates off guard, disarming their rehearsed responses and providing a glimpse into how they think. If they come up with an insightful question and answer, it tells me a lot about their self-awareness and depth. If they struggle or say "nothing," that also tells me something worth considering.

Who Do You Want to Hire? Who Do You Want to Work For?

Every company values Champagne, White Wine, and Red Wine hires differently. Some organizations prioritize flashy sales stars, while others thrive on stability or long-term innovation. ***Understanding where you fit and recognizing the kind of people you want around you can be the key to building a fulfilling career and a high-performing team.***

So, ask yourself: Are you hiring for the short-term splash or the long-term impact? And more importantly, who do you want to work for?

Chapter 3

Look in the
Mirror on 5th Ave

Whether in sales, leadership, or any career, the most successful professionals consistently invest in networking, both internally and externally. They build meaningful relationships through genuine, effective communication, and this skill often outweighs business acumen, hard work, or strategic positioning.

Your career growth isn't dictated by the company you work for, your clients, or the culture of your organization. It's entirely on you. The connections you build today will shape your opportunities tomorrow.

Many people make the mistake of focusing only on internal networking, aiming to navigate office politics or impress leadership. While internal relationships matter, they are inherently limited by company changes, restructures, and shifting priorities. Those who rely solely on internal positioning will eventually find themselves sidelined when the organization evolves beyond them.

Your external network is your real career insurance. A strong external network means that when you transition to a new company, your clients trust you, respect your expertise, and may even follow you. This trust is your true net worth. It allows you to control your career trajectory rather than be at the mercy of internal company dynamics.

Stay Focused on Your Own 5th Avenue

Imagine yourself walking down 5th Avenue in New York City. The distractions are endless: bright storefronts, people making flashy purchases, and tempting detours pull your attention in every direction.

Your career is no different. Office gossip, short-term wins, and internal politics may seem important at the moment, but they are distractions. If you lose focus on your three key priorities: excelling in your role, building an internal network, and cultivating an unprecedented external network, you'll veer off course.

The most successful professionals don't get distracted by the noise. They walk straight down the center of their own Fifth Avenue, watching the reflections in the storefronts, not to see others but to stay focused on what *they* are doing and how they're showing up.

Stay focused. Keep building. Keep walking.

Chapter 4

Bounce

Success in your career isn't about staying in one place. It's about learning, growing, and building a trusted network. Don't be afraid to bounce, whether that means shifting roles within your company or moving to a new organization. A career path doesn't need to be a straight line; sometimes, the best moves are lateral or unconventional. What matters most is the value you gain and the value you bring.

Internal Moves: Follow the Revenue

When considering an internal move, always assess how closely your role aligns with the company's top-line revenue. If your position doesn't contribute directly to growth, you'll always be vulnerable to restructuring, budget cuts, or shifting priorities. The closer you are to driving revenue, the more indispensable you become.

Your direct manager plays a pivotal role in determining your internal mobility. Before making a move, recognize what type of leader you'll be working under. Here are three common leadership archetypes:

- The Puppet: Just a mouthpiece for their boss

or the organization. They lack true leadership and are unlikely to advocate for your growth.

- The Politician: They move with the wind, always looking out for their own interests. Their support is conditional, shifting based on what benefits them at the moment.
- The Puncher: The leader you want. They fight for their team, push you to grow, and challenge you to be better. They won't always be easy on you, but they'll help propel your career forward.

These are broad categories, but your manager will define your experience. Before making an internal move, ask yourself: *Which category does my potential new manager fall into?* The answer could make or break your next step.

External Moves: The Blindfold Test

Moving to a new organization is trickier. You won't fully understand its true culture until you're inside. That's why you need to do your research, both before and after the interview process.

A key question to consider:

Does the company genuinely trust its employees, and do the employees truly value the organization?

A strong organization operates as if everyone were blindfolded. Trust, processes, and culture should be so strong that employees and leadership would still make the right decisions even if no one were watching.

A simple way to test this? Observe how the company handles mistakes. When something goes wrong, do they:

- Examine their processes and product first? This indicates a problem-solving culture where leadership takes responsibility.
- Immediately blame an individual or team? This suggests a culture of deflection, where the organization lacks the will or knowledge to improve.

Most employees are doing their best within the framework they're given. If an organization always blames individuals instead of fixing flawed processes or weak products, it's a red flag.

Your Career is a Series of Strategic Bounces

Every move, internal or external, should be strategic.

Bounce with purpose. Seek out environments that align with your skills, values, and long-term growth.

Stay close to revenue, choose the right leaders, and test the culture before you commit.

When you move wisely, you're not just changing jobs; you're building a career that lasts.

Chapter 5
Executives and Exits

If everything seems like rainbows and sunshine, run. That's not reality, and that's okay. Every organization, like every person, has struggles. The key difference is whether leadership acknowledges those struggles, addresses them openly, and takes action to improve.

When evaluating a company or deciding whether to stay with your current employer, pay attention to two critical litmus tests: The Executive Ego Test and The Exit Test.

The Executive Ego Test

Executives set the tone for an organization. Who they prioritize, themselves or their employees, tells you everything.

- If leadership is constantly name-dropping people and places, they are more focused on their own ego than the success of their employees.
- If leaders spend more time cheerleading than strategizing, jumping up and down with pompoms instead of providing a clear vision, chances are they don't have a real plan for success.

The executives you want to work for are more focused on nurturing talent than boosting their own image. They don't just tell employees how great they are. They follow it up with a roadmap for continuous improvement, openly discussing past mistakes and how to move forward.

If your top executives were placed by a private equity firm or hedge fund, recognize that their primary focus is ROI, not the product, process, or people. These leaders are typically short-term operators driven by returns, not long-term sustainability. That's not inherently bad, but it's critical to understand their motives.

The Exit Test: How They Handle Departures

How a company treats departing employees, especially those who performed well but are choosing to leave, can tell a lot about its culture.

- Do they thank employees for their contributions and send them off with respect?
- Do they treat them like a close relative heading off on a new adventure, wishing them well, keeping the door open for future collaboration?
- Or do they treat them like a cheating spouse, cutting ties, discrediting their work, and pretending they never existed?

The way a company handles exits reflects the value they truly place on employees, not just the ones retiring or achieving extraordinary success, but everyone.

Final Thought: Watch the Executives and the Exits

The executives and the exits will always reveal a company's true colors. Pay attention to both. They will tell you whether you are in the right place or it's time to make your next move. If you can't uncover meaningful insights from the core principles outlined above, there are two additional indicators worth paying close attention to.

First, the misuse of "Reply All" in email threads is a corporate canary in the coal mine. When employees regularly hit "Reply All," it often signals deeper dysfunction: either they're being micromanaged or they lack the situational awareness to respect others' time. In either case, it reflects a culture trending toward inefficiency and internal decay.

Second, meeting mismanagement is another red flag. If you walk out of a key meeting without a clear call to action, you should question why the meeting happened at all. Time is your most valuable, non-renewable asset. Every meeting should end with a simple but essential directive or question:

"Who is doing what, by when?"

If that isn't stated clearly, you didn't have a meeting; you had a time theft.

Chapter 6

Poker

In poker, position matters. Where you are at the table and how much information you've gathered before acting is critical. The preceding chapters are designed to equip you with key ideas, truths, and guidelines, all of which aim to put you in the best position to excel.

Now it's up to you. If you've ever watched or played poker, you'll notice players asking questions and closely observing each other, all to gather intelligence before making a move. One common mistake? Jumping straight for the jugular with a closed-ended question, much like an unskilled salesperson. Do you have a pair of tens? This is a direct question that can be answered with one word or a blank stare. These types of questions generally are not going to solicit the information that will be of value to you. How about instead, starting with a question that most likely will be answered with more than one word. Why would you make that move with only a pair of tens?

Opened-Ended vs Closed-Ended

This is one of the sacred rules of communication and sales. Ninety percent of your questions should be open-ended questions, not until the 9th question should you ever ask a closed-ended question and only if that closed-ended question is going to give you a result you would rate at least a 9 out of 10. Always remember the rule of 999's in sales and communication and the results you are looking to achieve will fall into your lap.

This chapter highlights the critical importance of positioning in poker, sales, and communication. Just as skilled poker players observe and gather information before acting, great salespeople should resist the urge to jump in with direct, closed-ended questions. These rarely yield meaningful insights. Instead, focus on asking open-ended questions, which invite dialogue and uncover useful details.

This is where the Rule of 999s comes in:

- 90% of your questions should be open-ended
- A closed-end question should never occur until at least your 9th question
- You should only use a close-ended question if it's likely to deliver a result that's a 9 out of 10 in value.

Equally important is the power of speaking last. When you let others talk first, you gather more context, uncover hidden motivations, and adjust your message with precision. Speaking first may feel assertive, but it often leaves you with less information. Those who speak last operate from a position of strength. By then, they've heard everything needed to highlight precisely what matters most.

———

Chapter 7
The Triangle of Life

Success in sales and life starts with effective questioning. The way you ask questions determines how much trust you build, how much information you gather, and ultimately, how successful your interactions will be.

The Wrong Way to Start

We've all been on the receiving end of a bad question, the kind that instantly puts up a wall instead of opening a door. One of the most common offenders in a social gathering we have all experienced is:

"Where do you work?" or *"Tell me about what you do."*

Yes, the second question is an open-ended question, but it's too direct and too impersonal. It doesn't create an immediate connection, nor does it guide the conversation in a meaningful direction.

The Upside-Down Triangle Approach

A far more effective method is the Upside-Down Triangle a structured way of building comfort and trust before diving into specifics.

Step 1: Start Broad and Non-Threatening

Your goal in the first phase is to get the other person comfortable talking. A good opener might be:

"I've done some research on your firm, but in your own words, can you give me a high-level overview?"

At this stage, resist the urge to interrupt even if something needs clarification. Let them speak. Take notes. The key is to allow the conversation to flow naturally.

Step 2: Narrow the Focus

Once they've shared the broad overview, slowly drill down:

"Tell me about your department and how it fits into the company's goals."

Then, go even deeper:

"Within the department, what is your role, and how do you operate within the team?"

Each question moves the conversation from macro to micro, guiding them deeper while keeping them engaged.

Step 3: Targeted Exploration

Now that they're comfortable, start uncovering specific pain points and opportunities.

For example, if you're discussing a competitor's product:

"It's my understanding that your team is using [Competitor X]. Can you share how and why you're using it?"

This is where the real insights come out the details that will help you craft a solution later.

The Big Mistake: Speaking Too Soon

One of the biggest errors salespeople make is jumping in too early with solutions.

For example, if a prospect says:

"One of the reasons we use Competitor X is because it comes in green."

An unskilled salesperson will immediately reply:

"Our product comes in green too!"

But that's a trap! You've now turned the conversation into a feature comparison rather than focusing on the real decision-making factors. Instead, keep listening, gather all the information, and only present a solution when you fully understand their needs.

Applying the Triangle to Presentations

Once you've gathered the necessary insights, the same Triangle approach should guide your presentation.

- Start Broad:
  - Recap the agenda and timeline.
  - Give a high-level overview of your firm.
  - Ask: *"Before we move forward, do you have any questions about our company?"*
- Narrow the Focus:
  - Discuss how your department fits into the organization.
  - Ask: *"Does this overview align with what you expected?"*
- Get Specific:
  - Explain your role and how you will support them.
  - Present the product/service and tie it back to their specific needs.
  - Ask: *"What feedback do you have so far?"*
- Confirm Along the Way:
  - After each section, check for clarity.
  - Instead of waiting for one big "yes" or "no" at the end, get buy-in throughout the conversation.

Know When to Walk Away

If you've executed the Triangle approach correctly, the ideal outcome is the prospect saying:

"That makes sense, and I'm excited to move forward with the next step."

But what if that moment never comes?

You have to recognize when you're wasting time on an opportunity that isn't real. Some prospects will never make a change until they're forced to. If you're not getting clear, engaged feedback, it may be time to move on.

Time is your most valuable asset. Don't waste it on people/organizations who aren't ready to act.

Final Thought: Master the Triangle, Master the Process

The Upside-Down Triangle isn't just a technique it's a mindset. Whether you're meeting a potential client, interviewing for a job, or networking, the same principles apply:

- Start broad; build trust first.
- Drill down; gather insights before acting.
- Confirm along the way; never assume agreement.

Master this, and you'll always control the conversation, uncover real opportunities, and close with confidence.

Chapter 8

The Smoke Screen

Objection handling is one of the most manageable parts of the sales process, provided you recognize what's real and what's a distraction.

The fact that a prospect is giving you objections is actually a good sign. It means they're engaged in the conversation. However, objections are often smoke screens, which are ways to deflect or stall rather than genuine roadblocks to buying.

Two Key Rules for Handling Objections

Rule #1: Never say, *"That's a good question/point."*

It may seem harmless, but if you say it once, you've set an expectation. If you don't say it for the next question/point, the prospect might subconsciously wonder, *Was my second question/point not good enough?* This can create unnecessary friction. Instead, acknowledge and confirm their question/point to maintain a positive and fluid conversation. This also demonstrates you are truly listening to their concerns.

Rule #2: Validate whether the objection is real or just a smoke screen.

Many objections are not the real issue. They're a way for the prospect to regain control of the conversation or delay a decision.

Spotting the Smoke Screen

Example:

A prospect says, *"I would buy your product if it came in green."*Most salespeople might rush to respond, *"Our product does come in green!"* thinking they've just overcome the objection.

Wrong move.

Before jumping to a solution, test the objection.

You: *"If we could provide the product in green, would we be able to move forward with our agreed upon next step?"*

- If they say yes, that's a valid objection.
- If they hesitate or pivot to another concern, you now know that *green* was never the real issue—it was just a smokescreen.

At that point, keep probing:

You: "I understand. Aside from color, what else would you need to feel confident moving forward?"

The real objection will eventually surface, whether it's price, timing, or internal politics. ***Until you find it, don't waste time solving false objections.***

When to Address the Objection

Another mistake salespeople make? Addressing objections too soon.

Even after validating the real objection, don't rush to solve it immediately. Continue gathering intelligence until you've uncovered all the decision-making factors. Objections should be addressed strategically within your presentation, not scattered throughout the conversation.

By waiting, you accomplish three things:

- You stay in control of the conversation.
- You ensure the prospect sees the full value before anchoring on one issue.
- You avoid playing objection whack-a-mole, where every answer just leads to another concern.

Owning the Sales Process

If you can't control the timing and agenda of the conversation, it becomes incredibly difficult to showcase the full value of your product or service.

Every sales process is full of smoke screens. Your job is to see through the haze, find the real objections, and address them at the right time.

Control the conversation, and you'll control the sales process.

Chapter 9
TP - When It Hits the Fan

Your next sale doesn't happen when you close a deal. It occurs after the sale. Post-sale is where you earn referrals, and past buyers turn into future buyers when they move to a new company and bring your product or service with them. But here's the reality: your best chance to build trust isn't when things are going well; it's when something goes wrong.

When the product, process, or people fail to meet the customers expectations, it's your moment of truth. The question is: Are you bringing the TP to clean up the mess?

TP = Trusted Partner

Any salesperson, account manager, or relationship manager can look like a star when everything runs smoothly. However, the real differentiator, the difference between transactional salespeople and true Trusted Partners, is how you handle unexpected problems.

When an issue arises, there are only two ways to respond:

- Backpedal and deflect: making excuses, blaming others, or disappearing when things get complicated.
- Step in and solve the problem: Own the issue, find solutions, and stand by your customers when they need you most.

If you take the first route, you'll lose that customer forever. They'll never buy from you again, and they certainly won't refer you.

But if you prove yourself as a Trusted Partner, you won't just keep the business; you'll earn long-term loyalty and advocacy.

Problems = Sales Opportunities

Most people see customer problems as headaches. Trusted Partners see them as sales opportunities.

When you step in and actively work toward a solution, you demonstrate your value beyond the initial sale. You show that you're invested in your customer's success not just in closing the deal.

Handled correctly, these moments can actually strengthen relationships, turning a dissatisfied customer into a lifelong advocate.

Who Shows Up When It Hits the Fan?

Now, let's flip the script. What about your company? Your colleagues? Your leadership?

Customers expect you to show up when things go wrong. But what about the people you work for and with?

- Do they only step in when the problem becomes too big to ignore?
- Do they disappear when things get tough?
- Or are they consistently present and engaged, even when things are going well?

A real Trusted Partner, whether a company, a leader, or a colleague, shows up consistently, not just when things blow up. If someone only engages when they're forced to, they're not a Trusted Partner; they're just covering their own interests

Final Thought: Be the TP, Not the Backpedaler

When a problem arises, you have a choice: be the Trusted Partner who finds a solution or be the one who disappears.

Customers never forget how they were treated when things went wrong. If you step up, take responsibility, and solve problems, you'll earn referrals, repeat business, and an external network that makes your career recession-proof.

And when evaluating the people around you, whether it's your boss, your team, or your company, ask yourself:

Do they act like Trusted Partners, or do they only show up when it benefits them?

If it's the latter, don't just play harder; play smarter. Find a better table.

Chapter 10

Process, Product, and People

Success in any organization, whether you're in sales, leadership, or operations, rests on three foundational pillars: Process, Product, and People. Picture a three-legged stool. If one of these legs falters, the stool collapses. But when all three are strong, the structure can withstand pressure and scale.

The Order of Evaluation: Process → Product → People

When turbulence hits, whether it's a sales slump, customer dissatisfaction, or internal conflict, the first instinct should be to assess the Process and the Product, not blame the People.

- Process: Are systems in place that set employees up for success? Are inefficiencies preventing growth?
- Product: Does the offering genuinely provide value, or is it outdated, overpriced, or misaligned with customer needs?
- People: Only after evaluating the first two should leadership turn their focus to individuals. If the same issues persist despite

a solid process and product, then it may be a people problem.

The best organizations fix problems in this order. Unfortunately, many take the opposite approach: blaming employees first without improving the underlying system.

Positioning Yourself for Success: The Power of Product

As a salesperson, your success is directly tied to the product you sell. If the product is weak, even the best sales skills won't save you in the long run.

Consider how your product is sold and valued:

- Low-Margin, High-Volume Products → Competing on price means you're in a race to the bottom. Over time, competition and customer expectations will drive margins so low that top salespeople won't be able to make a sustainable living.
- High-Margin, Value-Driven Products → Selling based on ROI rather than cost creates lasting value for customers and stronger compensation for salespeople.

The key question: **Does your product sell on value, or is it just a price game?**

If it's the latter, move on. You can have all the passion in the world for a product, but if it doesn't sustain long-term value, it won't sustain your career either.

Final Thought: ***Align with Stability, Growth, and Value***

Your success in sales or leadership depends on how well Process, Product, and People align. If you're constantly battling broken systems, a weak product, or poor leadership, you're in a losing game.

Instead, seek an environment where:

- The process is designed for efficiency and scale.
- The product is valued for its impact, not just its price.
- The people are trusted and empowered to succeed.

When all three are strong, the stool stands firm. So does your career.

Chapter 11

Give Value, Get Value

The core principle woven throughout this guide, whether in Mastering Context (TPO), Recognizing Talent, Networking, Managing Objections, or Becoming a Trusted Partner, boils down to one essential truth:

Give Value, Get Value.

A successful career in sales, or any relationship-driven profession, isn't about aggressively pushing your agenda. It's about consistently providing meaningful value to the people you engage with. In return, they will grant you something even more valuable: their time, trust, and insights.

Let's break this down and connect it back to everything covered so far.

Give Value First – It's the Fastest Path to Influencing Results

If you want to be heard, respected, and given access to decision-makers, you must bring something valuable to every interaction.

- This doesn't mean just selling a product or service. Giving Value can take many forms:
- Industry Insight: Sharing relevant trends or competitive intelligence that they may not be aware of.
- Personalized Expertise: Offering strategic advice based on your experience that genuinely helps their business.
- Connections & Introductions: Facilitating valuable introductions within your network.
- Efficiency & Convenience: Streamlining processes, making their job easier.
- Empathy & Understanding: Simply listening, asking insightful questions, and genuinely caring about their needs.

Every touchpoint with a client, prospect, or colleague should leave them with something useful, no matter how small. Over time, this builds your reputation as someone who adds value, not just extracts it.

Think about the concepts from TPO. The right kind of value depends on the Time, Place, and Occasion.

If you're at a casual networking event, sharing a strategic industry tip might be the best approach. If you're in a high-stakes negotiation, simplifying a complex decision-making process for your prospect could be the most valuable thing you can do.

__The most successful professionals don't ask,__
__"What can I get from this meeting?"__
__They ask, "What can I give?"__

Getting Value – The Art of Intelligence Gathering

While giving value is essential, it's only half of the equation.

The second part of this mantra, Getting Value, is about systematically gathering insights that advance the sales process.

Sales Intelligence Comes in Small Bits

The reality is, your prospect isn't going to give you every piece of information you need in one conversation. Instead, your job is to collect tiny, incremental pieces of intelligence over time.

Where can you Get Value?

- During appointment scheduling: What are their priorities right now? What internal challenges are they dealing with?
- In pre-meeting small talk: What personal insights can you gather? Any mutual connections?
- From the receptionist, assistant, or junior team members: How does the company really operate behind the scenes?

- In casual conversation after the meeting: How do they feel about your competitors? Their team dynamics?
- Through follow-up emails and texts: What responses or delays tell you about their level of interest?

Gathering value isn't just about asking questions. it's about active observation, listening, and reading between the lines.

Remember The Triangle of Life?

Your questioning strategy should move from broad to specific. The goal isn't to interrogate; it's to create a conversation in which your prospect naturally reveals insights that help you tailor your approach.

Every interaction should advance your understanding of their world, even if it's just a tiny piece of the puzzle.

The Balance: One Without the Other Fails

The power of Give Value, Get Value is in the balance.

If you only Give Value without Getting Value, you become a free consultant, useful but easily forgotten. You'll struggle to move deals forward because you're not uncovering the intelligence needed to close a sale.

If you only Get Value without Giving Value, you become a transactional salesperson who is purely self-serving. Your prospects will see through it, and over time, they will limit your access.

The key is to make every interaction a two-way exchange.

Give Value → Get Value → Repeat.

Master this rhythm, and you'll find that:

- You always have access to decision-makers.
- People seek your input and trust your insights.
- Your sales conversations become more natural and productive.
- You move deals forward with less friction.

Practical Application: How to Implement This Daily

To build this habit, start by adopting this mindset in your daily interactions:

- Before a meeting: *What specific value can I provide today?*
- During a conversation: *Am I balancing giving and getting value?*
- After every interaction: *What did I learn that moves this forward?*

Use the "The Rule of 999s"

90% of your questions need to be open-ended questions. If you've asked at least nine open-ended questions, only then should you consider a direct, closed-ended question, but the resulting value of this closed-ended question must be at least a 9 out of 10.

Most sales professionals focus too much on closing and not enough on value exchanges. But the best deals don't happen because of a great closing pitch. They happen because of a series of valuable interactions that build trust, credibility, and understanding.

Final Thought: The Give Value, Get Value Mindset

The core message of this guide, whether you're hiring talent, navigating career moves, handling objections, or positioning yourself as a Trusted Partner, is that sales is about relationships, not transactions.

Give Value, Get Value is not just a sales strategy. It's a way of operating in business and life.

If you consistently provide something meaningful in every interaction, people will instinctively open up, trust you, and ultimately, partner with you.

And that is how you win, not just in sales but in every professional and personal relationship.

Closing Note

Thank you for investing your time in reading this guide. I hope that it delivers insight and real, practical value you can use immediately, whether you're closing a deal, building a team, or navigating a conversation that matters. If this guide helped you think differently, communicate more effectively, or elevate your approach to sales and relationships, I'd be grateful if you shared it with a colleague, friend, or anyone who might find it valuable. After all, giving value doesn't stop with a conversation; it continues when we pass it on.

Acknowledgments

To my family, you three are my role models in life,
morning, noon, and night.
With all my love.

Author

Chris Whiting is an enterprise sales and leadership executive with deep, hands-on experience across financial software, SaaS, and API-based solutions. He has led complex enterprise sales and customer success organizations throughout the U.S. and Canada, earning a reputation for disciplined execution, consultative selling, and trusted executive relationships.

As a trusted advisor, coach, and author of *Give Value, Get Value*, Chris helps leaders and teams translate strategy into action, align technology to real business outcomes, and build durable relationships that drive long-term growth.

If you are exploring coaching or advisory support for yourself or your team, please reach out to my Executive Assistant, Sharon Bell, at Sharon.Bell@GiveValue-GetValue.com. Sharing a short overview of what you are working through will help guide next steps.
Should we schedule a conversation to see how I can be helpful?

Copyright © 2025 by Chris Whiting

Give Value, Get Value® is a federally registered trademark of Chris Whiting

Library of Congress

Paperback ISBN 979-8-9989522-8-9

Hardback ISBN 979-8-9989522-7-2

All rights reserved.

No part of this book/guide may be reproduced in any form or by any electronic or mechanical means, including information storage and retrieval systems, without written permission from the author, except for the use of brief quotations in a book review.

DISCLAIMER

This publication contains the opinions and ideas of its author. It is intended to provide helpful and informative material on the subjects addressed in the publication. The information contained within this book/guide is strictly for educational purposes. The strategies outlined in this book may not be suitable for every individual, and are not guaranteed or warranted to produce any particular results. If you wish to apply ideas contained in this book, you are taking full responsibility for your actions. This book is sold with the understanding that the author and publisher are not engaging in rendering any kind of personal professional services in the book.

The author and publisher specifically disclaim all responsibility for any liability, loss or risk, personal or otherwise, which is incurred as a consequence, directly or indirectly, of the use and application of any of the contents in this book. The author and publisher does not assume and herby disclaims any liability to any party for any loss, damage, or disruption caused by errors or omissions, whether such errors or omissions result from accidents, negligence, or any other cause.